THE SCARLET LETTERS

How to Save Yourself from Losing
Money, Time, Job, Sanity,
and Life as You Know It!

Natalie Hawthorne, RN

First Edition 2019

Printed in the United States of America

Published by: Creative Consulting Network
info@creativeconsultingnetwork.com
media@creativeconsultingnetwork.com
(909) 419-5520

Marketing, Editing, and Cover by Rory Carruthers Marketing
www.RoryCarruthers.com

This book is dedicated to all of those who do not have a healthy way to cope, whose only known coping skills are through alcohol and drugs.
My way of coping is through writing and helping others. I thank the universe for this skill and outlet that allows me to give back.

Contents

Introduction

Everything in this book is based on my experience and in conversations I have had with many professionals. Nothing should be interpreted as legal advice. This book has been written before any initial hearings with the DMV, BRN (Board of Registered Nursing), or the court system. There may be inaccuracies of inferred information. Everything in this book is reported to the best of my recollection, knowledge, and research; it does not at all discount or remove the human emotion or opinion that goes hand in hand with a matter this serious.

DUI/DWI does not discriminate, and nobody is immune.

You could be wearing a suit, a nurse uniform, ripped jeans, or a ball gown; you could be male or female, a celebrity always out in the limelight, or someone who rarely goes out in any light. This book is for those who have heard that getting a DUI is a "bad thing" and expensive but don't realize the magnitude of the consequences, regardless of the circumstances. My circumstance was innocent enough. I did not get pulled over or get in an accident, yet the consequences are the same.

Had I not attempted to take a friend home, I would not be writing this book. However, I firmly believe that everything happens for a reason. The universe has mysterious ways of solving this big puzzle called life. If this book was meant to be written to help even just one person in Anywhere, USA avoid a fatal crash or avoid wearing the brand of the Scarlett Letters, then this is the reason why this book had to be written. I will never know the outcome of how this book helped anyone specifically, but my story had to happen in order to prevent yours.

Chapter 1

A Day Like Any Other?

Hell starts the minute the officer says, "Step out of the car!" The abrupt halt in time, the humiliation, the sobriety testing, getting very tightly handcuffed to the point of swelling hands and wrist trauma, the ride to jail, not being allowed to pee for hours, the mug shot, the fingerprinting, and the indefinite period of time you will spend in jail after the initial arrest seems like punishment enough. But wait, that is just the beginning.

Christmas and New Year had passed, in addition to another month and a half, and I had been home every night working to reach my goals with my new business ventures and complete the books that I am writing. *This* book happened to come up unexpectedly.

I had been working my butt off for months with

my two businesses. My accountability coach even thinks I work too much. She and I both wanted me to go and have a night out. We both knew I deserved it.

It was a day like any other. I was working on two of my businesses, one of which is in healthcare. I am a Registered Nurse licensed by the Board of Registered Nursing who is connected to the Department of Consumer Affairs.

I am also branding an affirmation water product for those who believe in the power of affirmations, visualizations, and the power that you have within to control your destiny by asking the universe for what you want by visualizing and really *feeling* the emotions you want to come to fruition.

The "Affirmation Water Challenge" is something I am developing for the general public; however, it is a challenge I must experiment with first on myself in order to develop a program. That fateful day, I was on day 17 of my challenge and really noticed a huge difference in my demeanor, outlook on life, energy level, and ability to get things accomplished. I was challenging myself to live in gratitude and to make it part of my everyday routine, thinking in terms of gratitude with water at the helm as a tool and a reminder.

When I first started the challenge and made my first video journal entry, I was kind of lost. I made a video in the beginning, middle, and end to visualize the change I could see in myself. In addition, I also wrote journal entries every day to build positive momentum.

Here's my journal entry during the challenge on day 17:

> *Day 17 of 30. Friday.*
> *Made a video recording today. Just feeling more accomplished and ready to accomplish*

more. There has been a positive shift. A change is coming. It already has but will continue.

It was a simple yet definitive entry about the shift I was feeling. I was happy enough that I wanted to treat myself to something I really enjoy. It may sound cheesy, but I am a singer, and I love to go out and sing karaoke. It had been months since I had been out, and my exercises in affirmation and gratitude were creating a massive positive shift. I was feeling happier, more accomplished, and wanting to celebrate this victory. It's great to celebrate your victories no matter how big or small. We never give ourselves enough credit. Celebrating something, no matter how small, is something that pushes us up the ladder of gratitude and success by knowing what it is to graduate from smaller victories to bigger ones.

This was an important part of that day. This concept is meant to create positive shifts and momentum for not just myself, but eventually other people. What happened to me on this day occurred for a reason. Perhaps I do not know the entire reason yet; however, I can venture to guess that this book was meant to be written. Since you are reading it, it is specifically for YOU, so open your heart and mind and listen to the message it brings.

We have the power to change ourselves from within. The effect emotion has on water and our bodies (because our bodies are 80% water) was an experiment first done by Dr. Masaru Emoto back in the 1970s and is what started my quest delving further into what scientists are experimenting with today regarding his theory.

The "Affirmation Water Challenge" works physically and emotionally. It encourages you to drink more water and increase thoughts of gratitude while shaping your life with outcomes you pre-determine. One is a reminder of the other, and the water product is a tool to remind you of this throughout the day.

For those of you who are new to the power of gratitude, affirmations, and visualization to connect to what you want the universe to provide for you, let me briefly introduce you to Enhance Water.

This is my product; my tool. The premise is you enhance the water by thinking and stating affirmations (in the way of Dr. Emoto) while you are drinking it. Positive words are theorized to change the molecular structure of water into beautiful formations, such as the snowflake on the Masaru Emoto book cover. The theory is that since your body is made of 80% water, we can change the molecular structure of the entire body by saturating ourselves with the positive words and visualizations of what we want for our lives. In The Hidden Messages in Water, Emoto shares, "I believe I am also starting to see the way that people should live their lives. So how can people live happy and healthy lives? The answer is to purify the water that makes up 70 percent of your body."[1]

Some people practice this by writing affirmations on their own water bottles. Buddhists practice deep meditation. Enhance Water is an everyday tool we, as everyday Americans, can grab at the store or from our fridge on the way out the door. Instead of having to create new habits that may seem difficult, this is something right in front of you that you can easily use to get into a groove in your daily life. The label has affirmations on it, such as "I am grateful for my life" and "I can, I will, watch me!" and has space to write additional affirmations that are personal to you. For me, I have "I forgive myself" and "I am grateful," which

---

[1] Emoto, Masaru. *The Hidden Messages in Water*. Atria Books, 2005.

now will be replaced with "I can and will make positive and sound decisions in my life." It's positive infused water that becomes more positively infused by your own affirmations. Enhance your life one bottle at a time.

I used to sing in bands in where I live, especially at country clubs and corporate events. I missed that aspect of my life, so I decided to celebrate my happiness by doing the next best thing: KARAOKE! I got ready and, although it was snowing, decided to go out anyway. I have an all-wheel-drive car and no problem driving it. Away I went out by myself, anticipating running into the regular folks I always see no matter how much time goes by between my outings.

I made it out of the house early, around 6 p.m., so I stopped by the Elks club, of which I am a member. They do a lot of charity work in local communities. It's a wonderful way to meet a lot of great people who become friends, especially when you've been a member for thirteen years.

I started my night there so I could say hello to some happy, friendly faces. I decided to enjoy a

Greyhound, which is vodka and grapefruit juice. It's supposed to be the least sugary and low in calories. I was there for a couple of hours and ended up having two of those drinks along with the ice water I always have. A brother Elk was there needing a ride home. I knew I was fine, and he was not. The first mistake: I offered to take him home. As a registered nurse, it's only natural for me to instinctively help people. I should have taken him home first before going to sing. However, I took him with me to karaoke instead.

The snow continued. The conditions for most people would be sketchy, but I am used to driving in the snow and in other terrible conditions. So, for me and my all-wheel drive, this was a piece of cake. At 8 p.m. we arrived at the karaoke place to sing. I didn't want to spend the money on the small, expensive glasses of wine they had there. However, on second thought, the pours there are small, so if I got one glass, I would be OK to drive. After all, I was going to be there for a while. So, I decided to get a glass of wine and, in between, had several glasses of ice water, which is typical for me.

I got to sing a few of my favorite songs, and my ego was pumped up from the high fives and applause (ONE good thing had to happen right?). I now see where lack of judgment comes in. I was going to cash out, but the bartender asked if I wanted one more. For reasons I can't explain, I hesitantly said, "OK, one more, then close me out." This was approximately 11 p.m. Karaoke continued until 11:30 p.m., but a few of us hung around for another hour just chatting. Around 12:30 a.m., we walked across the parking lot to 7-Eleven, my friend I was taking home got a pizza, and then we got into my car.

My drive to take him home was the opposite direction of my house. While on the main highway approaching the left turn onto my friend's street, there was a CHP car blocking half the road. Importantly, not the half where I needed to turn. There was a car quite a bit ahead of me. That car turned left from the main highway where I was onto the side street halfway blocked by the police car. The police car had his yellow hazard lights on. I drove by the scene slowly to assess the situation and turned left past the road into a parking lot. We both agreed it looked like "caution ahead" and not a road closure because the half of the street I needed to drive on was open. It looked like a police car was warning drivers to approach with caution. I pulled out of the parking lot and turned right onto the street where it was open.

A few yards down, I had to stop because there was a tree that had fallen across the whole road. Ohhh, that's why the patrol car was there. Then the officer walked from his parked patrol car to my car. I was not nervous because I felt like I was OK to be driving. He asked some questions and asked to see my license, registration, and insurance. I told him I was driving my friend home because he was not able to drive himself. I'm not a good liar so when he asked me where I had been and how much I had to drink, I told him the truth: Elks 6 p.m., two greyhounds and the karaoke restaurant, two glasses of wine. It was now 1 a.m.

"Step out of the car, ma'am."

We then walk up to where his car was parked. He said, "Can't you tell the road is closed?" I know

I seriously gave him a weird look (not on purpose) because I was still baffled. I said, "No, this whole side of the road is open."

In addition to that, his SUV was parked directly in front of the road closed sign. The sign was a foot from his car in line with the driver side door. Nothing was blocking the entire street. I took a picture of the actual road closure the next day, but by then, it was then a proper road closure. Road closures are obvious. Seriously, I am not oblivious. There was no erratic driving, I didn't barrel through cones or signs like they do in the movies. I wouldn't have driven on the open side of the road if it was not open.

I did not get a ticket for anything else, meaning, I did not do anything wrong as far as my driving was concerned. I didn't even get a ticket for going through what he considered a road closure, probably because it was not closed properly. If the road had been closed properly, and I was ignoring that, I would have gotten a ticket.

Ahhh, but none of that matters.

The law is the law. If you're driving over the limit

of 0.08%, there is no escaping the consequences, regardless of the reason why the officer came to your window.

When I stepped out of the car, the road was at a slope, and there were a few inches of snow and slush on the road. It was freezing out. We were out there talking for at least an hour and a half. He was trying to have me perform field sobriety tests. When my ex-husband, who was a CHP officer, used to have me perform those tests randomly just to mess with me, without any drinks in my system, I could never do them. He thought it was funny. I had a spinal cord injury in my past and have myelopathy (spinal cord compression), which still affects my balance and fine motor coordination today. "Early symptoms of cervical myelopathy include changes in coordination or fine motor skills of the arms, weakness/numbness in the arms or legs, or problems with balance."[2]

I have a neurologist who gives me tests, and I

---

[2] Bjerke, Benjamin. "Cervical Stenosis with Myelopathy." *Spine*, www.spine-health.com/conditions/spinal-stenosis/cervical-stenosis-myelopathy.

cannot complete the balance tests without wobbling or catching myself on the wall. It's not like I just walk and fall down; however, it is very easy for me to lose my balance if I stand on one foot or lose my footing from a cracked sidewalk while walking.

I tried to explain this to the officer; however, I'm certain they hear so much bullshit all the time, it was hard for me to even say it to him with conviction. All I could think was, "he's thinking, 'yeah right whatever lady, you're a liar.'" He kept trying to make me do the tests anyway. I did not realize at the time that I could refuse them. "Sir, I cannot do these tests, I have balance issues, I won't be able to do any of them." He still kept making me do them, going from one to the next.

If you think you are below the legal limit, just refuse the field test and blow into the machine. You don't even have to blow into the machine in the field, but if you don't, you will be arrested and forced to do it at the station.

Had I known better, I would have said no to the field test. I did breathe into the machine in the field. He did not get a reading and said I was "doing it wrong." He only let me try once. He did not demonstrate the field tests to me. He didn't tell me what would be correct or incorrect. After I blew into the PAZ machine (the field breathalyzer), he never said he was taking me to jail. He never said much of anything. I thought I was doing another field test when he said, "Take your left hand and place it behind your head. Then take your other hand and place it behind your head." Suddenly, he put handcuffs on me!

It was very surreal. I really had no idea what he was thinking the entire time. He didn't even tell me where we were going. As we approached the town of Running Springs, I asked him if that was where we were headed. The answer was, "No, we are going down the mountain to San Bernardino."

The handcuffs were so tight, it left marks for two days and caused a hard lump to develop on my right wrist. As of right now, I also cannot lift anything with my left arm. I feel like a muscle or tendon has been torn. I am seeing the doctor tomorrow for it. It has been fourteen days, and I still haven't fully recovered from the swelling, pulled muscles and tendons, and pinched nerves caused by the handcuffs being so tight. That part was not necessary. Besides being mad at myself, I have to admit that I am angry about having suffered physical harm that still influences my everyday ability to perform routine things without extreme pain.

When you are nervous, it's freezing out, and three hours go by, there will be a point when you have to use the restroom. At the station with nerves building, I really had to go, to the point where I couldn't keep still. When you ask to use it, they aren't going to let you use it right away, even though there is one right there. What was actually happening was vague because I was literally going to pee my pants. Have you ever had to hold it to where you actually get pain in your bladder? That's where I was. He said something like, "Yeah, well I have to pee too; we're both in this situation because of you." He was alluding to the fact that is was my fault that I had to pee. I don't remember when a bodily function was my fault. It reminded me of my parents who blamed me for basically being alive and having bodily functions to take care of. It was really uncalled for and painful. I spoke to some lawyers who said that some officers try to deliberately make you pee your pants. This is the kind of horrifying treatment you get. All of this is what I am trying to prevent happening to YOU. It doesn't matter that you are a small female being cooperative. You are treated like the large, angry, combative, tattooed thug who just robbed a liquor store and ran.

Finally, when they let me go to the bathroom, it was in an open cell with two other girls in it with large plexiglass windows into other police rooms. Not one iota of privacy. Did I deserve that? I really was treated very poorly. I had no idea that I was now this level of criminal. Mind you, the entire time I did not say anything beyond telling him what I had to drink, telling him why I didn't think there was a road closure, and "yes" or "no" answers to everything else. Sometimes when he asked me something sarcastic, I just didn't answer. I was as polite as I could be because I respect their position. Even though I am innocent until proven guilty, to them I am guilty until proven otherwise. This just goes to show you that they can choose to be decent or not. In this case…not so much.

Once someone at the jail was finished asking a series of health questions and after I had been given two back-to-back breathalyzer tests, I was put back in the same cell with the two girls. Throughout the six hours, we were moved three times to three different holding cells for no particular reason. In the middle of all this, I was called into a room to get fingerprinted and have my mugshot taken. No one told me anything the whole time. I had no past criminal record and no marks on my driving record, not even a ticket. Let me assure you, none of this matters. Right now, you are officially a criminal.

Chapter 2

The Next Day

The total time spent from arrest to release can be anywhere from 9 to 27 hours. My total time was three hours in the field and the minimum six hours required in jail. A total of nine hours. I guess if I had been drunk or combative, they would have kept me the entire 24 hours in jail. They did let me out after the minimum. A good sign, possibly?

Once you are released, the expenses begin with the cab ride home. You can't get your car out of the tow yard until it is open, which might be a few days later. In my case, it was three days later. You will get your car back the day the shop opens, but don't think you are going to get it right away. No, you will get it when THEY are good and ready. If you call at 8 a.m. you will get your car at about 4 p.m. Believe me, the company works alongside the CHP when it comes to punishment. The tow company which is attached as a subcontractor to the CHP will punish you with time and money. By the time they are ready for you to pick up your car, you have a $700 bill on your hands. It's $300 per hour for the tow to go literally half a mile. They said it took an hour and thirty-eight minutes, which is rounded up to two hours. Plus three days of storage, even though I called at 8 a.m. first thing Monday morning.

While you try to get your car back, you will also want to get a lawyer. Calling around to shop for one makes you relive the horrible situation all over again. When you think you have the right one, the bill can be anywhere from $3,000-$8,500. Keep in mind, the cheapest representation is not always the worst, and the most expensive is not always the best.

Three days after my arrest, my total cost were:

Rental car plus gas	$ 150
Getting car out of impound	$ 670
Lawyer with trial insurance	$8,500
Grand total	$9,320

From the time of first contact with the officer until right now seems like torture enough. Yet, your punishment hasn't even begun. This cost does not even count the OTHER lawyer I require for the BRN which will be another $5,000 to $10,000. You will learn more about this later.

Do I feel like a criminal? Most certainly.

Getting arrested is not something anyone wants, especially a professional like myself. You can be a very upstanding citizen with a professional job and still be cuffed and thrown from the back of a police car into a dirty cement cell to sit on the floor for a period of time that is definitely indefinite.

DUI does not discriminate.

One minute you're having the time of your life at a party, at dinner, at karaoke, and the next minute, you're in the back of a police car.

Chapter 3

Your Life as You Know It Is Over

I spent Christmas and New Year at home by myself. So, when I say I hadn't been out in months, I mean I really hadn't been out. I'm not one of those people who go out on what other people call "amateur night." When I was young and lived in LA, I loved going out. I'm at a point in my life now where priorities have changed drastically.

I started my own business and to cover expenses while that is coming together, I was planning on working part-time in hospice. I started my own hospice work throughout my life when I seemed to step up to the plate with friends who needed help at home when a loved one was dying of cancer. It started with my friend Lance back in 2003 who had lung cancer. Then, in 2013, I spent a couple of weeks with a friend whose wife and two young kids really needed someone there full-time since the end of his life was coming. I was there when he died and helped clean him up and get him set for viewing by his children and friends who would celebrate his life at his home. When the hospice nurse arrived, she said, "Wow, you're a really good friend." I wasn't thinking that I was a good friend, I just did what needed to be done to help.

When my mother got sick in 2014, I moved back to New York and took care of her until the end. I felt like an only child because I did not get any help or contact from any of my siblings while I was making all of these heavy decisions and caring for her 24 hours a day. They wouldn't even answer my calls. They didn't want to do anything. When I told my older brother, an officer of the law, that I could use a day of respite, his answer via text was, "What's that?" and nothing more. It was the most difficult thing I have ever done because it was a 24 hour a day job, and it was my mother.

It was not only the hardest thing I ever did, but it was also in a strange way, the most gratifying. I felt like I participated in the second most important event in a person's life. Birth being the first, and death being the second. I find it to be a privilege to participate in helping with this most important transition in a person's life. That is why I really wanted to continue work in hospice so I could serve others in the same way I have served friends and family. My first-hand experiences allow me to bring empathy, compassion, and wisdom to others when they need it most. However, my ability to work as a nurse will be taken from me with the disciplinary action forever stamped onto my nursing license. Branded like a scarlet letter for something that did not have ANYTHING to do with my ability as a nurse.

It's so confusing. I went out to celebrate the good things happening in my life with some karaoke. According to the breathalyzer, my judgment was evidently altered. I drove a friend home who obviously should not be driving, and now my entire life is ruined. HOW did this happen? It's like living a nightmare that I will never wake up from. I just can't wrap my head around how this is going to affect my career as an RN or my ability to get or keep a job.

CHP officers don't have these intense ramifications, and they are the ones that uphold these laws. How am I, a nurse, held to a higher standard than the CHP who enforces the very law I am being arrested for? The $20,000 I needed for marketing and launching my new venture to help people is now being given to lawyers. In a nutshell, my life is over.

I did not get into an accident, I wasn't driving erratically, no one was hurt, yet the consequences are all the same. The only way the punishment would be one step worse is if I killed someone. There are no graduated steps where the punishment equals the crime. How did we come to this as a society? What happened was in no way related to my job as an RN, or a reflection of who I am as a person every other day of my life.

I have started nonprofits for fire victims, volunteered for end of life care for family and friends, I think of others always before myself…but this time, to my detriment by caring enough to give someone a ride home who was not ok when I felt I was.

Chapter 4

Intuition - Listen to It

I usually drink when I am happy versus trying to "drown my sorrows." I was particularly happy this day and really wanted to go out and sing! Singing is such a great release and something I love to do.

I believe wholeheartedly in listening to the universe, your gut instinct, your intuition, whatever you choose to call it. When it started snowing a lot, the thought crossed my mind, "Do you really think it's the best day to go out?" I quickly dismissed the thought and talked myself into all the reasons why I should go out. It's the initial, instinctive, seemingly "fleeting" thoughts that are your intuition. All I can say about that is ALWAYS listen.

How do you know it is your intuition? It's simple. If a thought comes to your mind about anything, this could be true for a relationship, something expensive you are thinking about buying, or in my case, something you set out to do, and you have that fleeting thought of doubt, and you have to talk yourself into all the reasons why you should not listen to that little voice in your head, that is how you know.

How many of us make excuses for a person we are dating when all the "red flags" come up? Red flags, my friends, are intuition. If you are listening to a salesperson, and you really want what they are selling, but something doesn't seem right with what they are saying, THAT is intuition. Here's the thing, you may never know the negative outcome that you avoided by listening to your gut. If you're dating a guy and you break up, you may hear through the grapevine that they put their hands on their next girlfriend, or you may never know anything at all. Had I listened to my gut instinct and stayed home, I would have never known the ensuing disaster I would have avoided. Nevertheless, I would have avoided this whole fiasco that will now have a negative impact on the rest of my life.

Here's another example for you of intuition at work. Quite a few years ago, I went on one date with someone. The date consisted of him coming to my house for dinner. He seemed amazing, almost too good to be true. Was he really this perfect? Things were so right that I thought, something isn't right here. Was this me trying to talk myself out of a good thing?

My instinct took over, and I posed the question right out of the blue: "Have you ever been to jail?" (OK, well now I have, but that's beside the point at the moment!) He not only said yes, but it was for something very big, and he was in for a long time. The conversation went downhill from there for me and seemingly uphill for him. His conversation turning into how he was "somebody" when he was in jail. That he had power and respect. It was his "time," almost a joyful time where he was at the top of his game because he was important in prison. Now did this scare me?

Actually, not really. I was fascinated by his conversation and asked questions. However, I CAN tell you that, although I did not instinctively have any sense that I needed to fear him or think he would break into my house later down the line, it was evident that, according to my instinct, there was something wrong. Did I ever go on a second date with him? Absolutely not. If he felt remorseful and felt like he learned from what happened and it changed his life for the better, I may have thought about it. However, this was more like Henry Hill in *Goodfellas* when he went into witness protection. He was SOMEBODY when he was in the mafia, and living a normal life of the everyday human was degrading and not for him.

So, my strong advice to you is when you have that little voice in your head, don't try to talk yourself into or out of what it's telling you. Just listen. You may never know what you avoided, but you are alive and well, with the same amount of cash in your pocket.

Chapter 5

The AA Meetings

Mind you, I have not been formally charged yet; however, I hired a lawyer initially in order to get with the DMV within ten days of arrest to avoid immediate suspension. The law firm highly recommended going to AA meetings because it would look good. This is a whole other hell and punishment of its own kind and may or may not make a difference in my case.

I am attending AA meetings online. It's a Zoom meeting, just like the big boys have in the business world. At the first meeting, there were about ten people present. They have them every week at the same time.

They have a guest speaker and a new topic every week, which made me choose this particular group. Perhaps they all run that way, but the explanation was specific in the information on the website, so I decided I would try this group.

Attending this really did make me realize how lucky I am as a human being. I do not have the problems these people have. Some of them have been in recovery for a while, so they have some nice input about life. Others are still in the middle of their struggles, and it negatively impacts every aspect of their lives.

Therein lies the confusion for me. I drank and drove unknowingly and unintentionally over the limit, and THAT is now affecting every aspect of my life. It's affecting my driving record, my criminal record, my professional licensure, and my career. Unlike those in AA, altering substances are not calling to me from the moment I wake up until I go to bed (if an alcoholic can even sleep from the torturous thoughts).

Attending this meeting made me realize whole-heartedly that I am not an alcoholic. Am I influenced by misjudgment when overindulgence is not recognized? Evidently, I was not aware that I overindulged. I felt good enough to drive my very inebriated friend home. I'm a nurse, that's what I do: help others out and put others first before me.

In essence where being an alcoholic may or may not impact all aspects of your life. You may hurt people because of it, lose jobs, money, status, all of it or none of it, whatever the case may be for each individual. The bottom line is that you can be an alcoholic and NOT have your life as screwed up as it gets by going out to have fun and getting behind the wheel. This is a very important concept to walk away with. You do not have to be an alcoholic or a criminal to have your life completely changed and ruined by something you were intentionally trying to avoid.

My second AA meeting made me realize that the topics are good for personal growth. I can relate to them and participate on that level. I just can't relate every feeling, incident, and problem back to alcohol. I can only relate to it on a fundamental human level. I am trying very hard to fit into these meetings; however, I really don't belong in this type of group. I would be much better off in a John Assaraf personal development group. I can always grow, learn, and be a better person. AA just seems to be bringing me down, makes me feel very bad for everyone else, and makes me feel like I have no business being there. Almost like I'm a mockery to their organization.

Knowing that I am not an alcoholic does not give me ANY solace whatsoever. These individuals who are true addicts may have a life that is in better shape than mine is now because they may not have a criminal record or a bad driving record. They may not have professional licensure that will be taken from them after four years in school, one year of studying for the professional exam, and thirteen years in practice. The takeaway here is that the self-labeling of "alcoholic" does not equal involvement with the law. Conversely, involvement with the law because of an alcohol-related event does not equal alcoholism and should not all equal a crime of the same magnitude.

Would I have been better off being an alcoholic who had not driven? Well, I'm not exactly suggesting that. It's merely a comparison between the two. One does not go hand in hand with the other. Going to the meetings makes you realize you aren't one of "them;" however, you are more closely associated on the scale of a bank robber in the criminal sense. Even robbing a bank doesn't affect your driving record, to my knowledge. Substance affiliation is the only thing that will affect your entire world. The financial aspect is devastating, you will lose your job, the ability to work in your profession anywhere, and you lose your driving privileges in the state where it occurred. Now you are branded a criminal and have to answer "yes" to any questions ever again about being one.

If I knew then what I know right now, I would have not gone out that particular evening, and I would always make sure to have $25 extra dollars and a lot of extra time for the cab ride home. The bare minimum of $20,000 I am going to be out of in this process would have paid for a lot of cabs or even getting my masters. I used to not go out if I did not have money to tip. Well, now cab money holds the same consideration.

When you go out and have any amount of

alcohol, not only do you need extra money for tipping, you need extra money for a taxi. It's that cut and dry. This is not something you want to have to go through and not something you ever have to guess if you are really OK, possibly on the edge, or below the limit. This is no time to be guessing. JUST DON'T DRIVE.

Regardless of the outcome at the DMV, the BRN, or the court, even if the case was dropped right now, the time, the money, the stigma, and the feeling that the punishment was already severe will prevent me from ever getting behind the wheel after having even ONE drink. I don't go out that much. I can spare an extra $25 for a ride, and if I can't, then I can't go out. Simple as that.

This has been hell on wheels, and I am still in the phase *before* the DMV hearing and *before* the court hearing AND before the Board of Registered Nursing (BRN) hearing. **The punishment does not fit the crime.** You have a trial with legal fees and punishment with the DMV inclusive of losing your driving privileges along with an SR-22 filing and increased insurance that may not be remotely affordable for at least three years.

Then you have the criminal trial with legal fees initially for the lawyer and then potentially triple if it goes to trial. That comes with its own set of fines, classes, AA and various other meetings that need to be paid for. The mark stays on your driving record for ten years. I don't know how long it stays on your criminal record. I think forever.

Then you have the BRN to deal with. Their "voluntary program" for the diversion program is 3-5 years at $10,000 a year. If you don't "volunteer," you have the disciplinary scarlet letters FOREVER on your professional license.

We are talking $25,000-$30,000 just for lawyers alone between the court, the DMV, and your professional license. In addition to this, I have a 50% tear to the ligament to my left elbow from the twisting injury of being handcuffed and a contusion and nerve damage to my right wrist from the same reason. I am going to have to pay for my doctor visits, MRI's, and months of physical therapy.

How does a nurse who was not driving

erratically, who was helping a friend get home, who would have safely gotten home otherwise get into a mess of this MAGNITUDE?

No one has to die or get hurt or permanently maimed for this to be the nightmare that it is. I couldn't imagine that ever happening with myself as the cause. I am hoping this saves even just one life, prevents an accident, but mostly, prevents anyone from having the experience I am having. Heck, if I can save one LICENSE, that will be enough, but if you're reading this you probably have two licenses at stake: driving and professional.

Even on the best day, you can inadvertently do something that brings your car to the attention of law enforcement. What if one of your lights is out? I was pulled over on a Friday night at 9 p.m. coming home from working in the NICU at Community Hospital San Bernardino. It was prime time for a weekend, so I was pulled over for my light being out above my rear license plate. What if I had been out? What if I had just one drink? I was coming home from work. All was well.

I wasn't planning on going out. However, you can get pulled over for something small and still end up in jail.

Chapter 6

What Happens to a Professional When They Get a DUI/DWI?

There is no prior knowledge or warning in nursing school or at your job. An RN does not know the ramifications of a DUI until it happens. As a professional, once you are given a professional license, you have to think of it not only as the valuable asset that it is, but always remember how hard you worked for it and what it took to get that license in your hand.

It's not just a license. You are representing your organization. It's something that needs to be held to the highest standard. Your behavior outside of work still reflects your position. This is something I never realized. This is not something we are taught in school. Is it supposed to be innate knowledge if you never had a role model in your life? Schools should not take anything for granted that human beings in any profession don't need personal development or something to strengthen their relationship to who they are really becoming and what they are representing in their profession. Even those who do not need to put on an official uniform. If you are a pilot or law enforcement, there is something about the uniform that makes the person who is wearing it more aware of what they represent. Whatever you wouldn't do in uniform, you shouldn't do when you're not. Seems like common sense, however, for nurses, we are in a class all our own.

We are punished every day we go to work (because it IS a punishing job), and we are punished harder than anyone else for things that can happen to anyone. Getting a DUI does not automatically make one an alcoholic. It also does not mean you are a criminal even though you are branded as one. Criminal by definition is one who breaks the law. That I am being accused of. However, we all get a picture in our head of what a "criminal" really is, and I know I would not fit that stereotype.

I never realized that, with whatever license you have, you are representing yourself, your community, and your profession. Having a criminal charge on your BRN license, or a license of any kind, is a complete disservice to yourself as a human being. When I was married to a CHP officer (which was probably the best part of my life), the department instilled self-respect and respect for the department and that you were a part of something BIG, a team, and a family. Some professions instill that in you, where others don't.

Nurses get hit the hardest when they get a DUI. Even harder than the CHP. Oh yes, CHP's are not exempt from the law like they used to be. It depends on who pulls them over. If a rival "gang" such as the Sheriff's department pulls them over, they may find some joy in arresting a CHP.

I know someone personally that this happened to. He was arrested and went through some of the things I've described. However, when it came to his work, he got two weeks suspension and two weeks of office duty. His penance was over. As far as his license goes, well, he's a CHP, so nothing really applied to him. There were little consequences there. He kept his license, and his charges were reduced in court.

When you have a CDL (commercial driver's license), you know that there is zero tolerance for drinking and maintaining your license. They are educated on that. They know it before it happens. With a nursing license, they don't even put you through a class to let you know what happens to you if you get a DUI. There are no CEU's (continuing education) to educate you on the facts or that updates you on anything new or changes in the BRN laws regarding alcohol offenses. How is it that you can be supposedly driving home over the limit, not even get stopped for doing something you shouldn't be, and suddenly you could lose your job altogether? It seems unconstitutional that a state board governing in the United States of America can pull a punch like that. The Board is ruthless. You only have a few choices. One option is the Diversion Program, "a voluntary, confidential program for registered nurses whose practice may be impaired due to substance use disorder or mental illness."[3] In this program, they have complete control over how long you are in, usually 3-5 years, and the cost is tens of thousands of dollars. If you do not volunteer into this program, you have a severe disciplinary mark for a lifetime on your record that is public domain. Again, the punishment does not fit the crime.

Registered nurses are referred to the Diversion Program by the BRN as a result of a complaint (being contacted by the agency who arrested you through electronic fingerprinting) indicating the RN may be impaired due to substance use disorder or mental illness. If a nurse chooses not to enter the program, the complaint is referred to the Enforcement Program for investigation and possible (more like probable) disciplinary action. I don't understand the assumption that someone who gets a DUI/DWI has a definite alcohol problem.

I received THE LETTER today. The letter I

---

[3] "What You Should Know About the BRN Diversion Program." *SEIU Nurse Alliance of California*, www.nursealli128ca.org/2015/02/02/what-you-should-know-about-the-brn-diversion-program/.

knew was coming because of a conversation with my lawyer, but somehow, it was still like a punch in the gut. It took the wind out of my sails.

STATE OF CALIFORNIA
BOARD OF REGISTERED NURSING
PO Box 944210, Sacramento, CA 94244-2100
P (916) 322-3350 F (916) 574-8637 | www.rn.ca.gov

March 6, 2019

> **Please respond within 14 days**

Dear

The Board of Registered Nursing (Board) has received information that may suggest your ability to practice is impaired due to substance use disorder (misuse or abuse of alcohol and/or drugs; other drug-related transgression) or mental illness. The Board is responsible for investigating this information to determine if cause exists to pursue disciplinary action against your RN license.

The purpose of this letter, however, is to inform you of an opportunity to participate in the Board's Intervention Program as an ALTERNATIVE to discipline.

The Intervention Program is a CONFIDENTIAL recovery monitoring program designed for eligible registered nurses, residing in California, who need help to recover from substance use disorder and/or mental illness. The Intervention Program's goal is to protect the public by ensuring an RN's safe return to nursing practice. The Program has proven to help many RNs achieve successful recovery and re-entry into nursing practice.

If you choose to VOLUNTARILY participate in the Intervention Program, you will have access to dedicated professionals who will assess your needs and develop an individual recovery plan for you. The Program will continually monitor your success in recovery as demonstrated by your participation and compliance with your individual plan. If you choose to participate in and successfully complete the Intervention Program, the Board will not take disciplinary action against your RN license.

HOW DO I ENROLL? Please contact MAXIMUS California Health Professionals Diversion Program staff at (800) 522-9198 to schedule an initial intake appointment.

ADDITIONAL QUESTIONS? We understand this may be a difficult decision. As such, if you would like to first discuss your options before enrolling, please contact Board Intervention Program staff within 14 DAYS at (916) 574-7692. We will not be able to discuss specific information the Board has received, but we can answer any questions you may have about the Intervention Program. You will also find additional information about the Intervention Program at the Board's website at www.rn.ca.gov/intervention.

Sincerely,

Kim Poston
Intervention Program Analyst

Enclosures

LTRIB (rev 12/3/2018) mdb

Since I have to trek to the post office to get my mail, I received it on a Friday. Monday was day 14. Great. I called the number to speak to the lady who is head of the diversion program to inform her that I am calling within the 14 day period but they have to wait until I finalize everything with my lawyer and he gets in touch with them.

Apparently, that was the wrong thing to say. When you talk to the police, you are supposed to say, "My lawyer told me not to say anything…" If you say that to the BRN, it only makes them mad. I was told that they needed to hear from me about the diversion program by Monday. If they don't hear from me, they will send another letter giving me five more days to respond. Then they will assume I am refusing, in which case, I have some kind of disciplinary mark on my license that lasts forever.

I spoke to a lawyer today who specializes in professional license matters. He said there is no way I am going to make it through the diversion program because you have to admit you are an alcoholic and are then treated as one with inpatient therapy. If you do the program to get out of the disciplinary action but say you are not an alcoholic, then they say you are in denial, and you won't pass the program. If you leave in the middle of the program or are dismissed for the reason I just stated, you are back to the disciplinary action on your license forever. I told the lawyer I could consider playing the game and lying through the program and just say I am an alcoholic. He said aside from the fact lying is not the greatest idea, he said people like me (who do not have a drug or alcohol problem) never make it through.

The reason why I didn't think I was over the limit may very well be because I was not. There are physical ailments that can cause readings to be higher and even double than normal. GERD (Reflux disease) is one of those medical conditions. In addition, the BAC machine cannot decipher between alcohol and acetone. You breathe out acetone when your blood sugar crashes to a low number. This typically happens in diabetics; however, I have severe reactive hypoglycemia. This means if I have sugar (or products that turn into sugar, such as alcohol) without eating a lot of food, my pancreas throws out all kinds of insulin, making my blood sugar crash. I was feeling funny during the stop the night I was arrested. Low blood sugar can cause slurring your words and other symptoms that could imitate having alcohol. I ate a small dinner before I went out and nothing for the rest of the night. Those drinks could have easily adversely affected me with reactive hypoglycemia. With that coupled with GERD, I could have easily blown a much higher result. I took the liberty of purchasing a breathalyzer to keep it in my car so that this never happens again, or so that I can help someone else by having it. Since I have medical conditions that can make a reading higher, that's even more reason NOT to ever drive if I imbibe. I could always incriminate myself with a much higher reading. Mind you, I only knew this after the fact from doing a lot of research.

I remember when my ex-husband first became a CHP officer years ago, we went to another CHP officer's house and stayed the night. They took a breathalyzer machine home so we could drink and experiment with it. It was a very interesting experiment because we drank three drinks over the course of a couple of hours and the last thing we did was a shot. He had us wait twenty minutes after each drink before blowing into it. We would take turns guessing what we thought our own reading would be. I was surprised at how much time and how many drinks it took before it registered above 0.08%. That experiment actually made me feel better about how much I could have and over what period of time in order to stay safe. Perhaps THAT machine was calibrated incorrectly or unknown factors were affecting it to make it read lower. This evidently is not an exact science. It made me feel safe with what I could drink in order to stay safe on the road; however, following that as my life guideline did not prove to be accurate. However, I did not have GERD or Severe Reactive Hypoglycemia back then.

According to what happened at this arrest, I had less over a longer period than when we did that experiment and blew over the limit. Since there is not an exact science and the machines are fallible, and with variables of medical conditions that cause higher readings, the only safe thing to do is NOT DRIVE at all. The oxymoron here is that getting caught drinking and driving is what labels you an alcoholic. I could go out every night, drink until I fall down, and as long as I get rides everywhere and don't drive, then I won't acquire that label.

Here's an opposite example: a friend of mine who is not in the medical field but has a good job, kids, a nice house, all the toys you could want (boat, jet skis, etc.), pays for nice things, and pays on time for everything tried to check himself into rehab because on his off time he drank 3-5 liters of rum a week. The rehab facility would not take him. He was not destitute. He was living life in a responsible manner. They turned him away, and he had to rely on the support from his girlfriend to help him stop on his own.

Then there's me. Someone who does not keep alcohol in the house regularly, goes out twice a month on a good month and has four drinks (usually less), and my whole life is flushed down the toilet. I might as well give everything up and go live under a bridge and shoot up every eight hours because that is what I am being treated like. My life as I know it is over. I don't understand it, and I don't see how it's the least bit constitutional. I was not stopped because I was driving erratically. I was not even pulled over. A police officer approached my car when I could not drive any further because a tree was down across the road. How am I living a nightmare? How has my life turned upside down? If I sound a little frantic, it's because I am, everyday.

Chapter 7

The Lawyer Nightmare

This is a very difficult journey in itself. Do I need a lawyer? Why is the right lawyer so imperative? How do you know if you have the right lawyer?

Well, truth is, you don't know if you have the right lawyer, but YES, you do need one. Again, you go with your intuition and send out a lot of prayers that you made the right choice. There are certain aspects, however, to look for. Of course, lawyers say to go with a lawyer who is strictly a DUI lawyer. My feeling in dealing with those who are strictly DUI is a little different. I personally like a good criminal lawyer who knows DUI law. Why? My personal opinion is that they think a little bit more outside the box when it comes to helping you and can personalize your strategy.

There's only so much you can do. Research and

research, look up reviews, have consultations, and eventually they all sound the same and no one really stands out. They all have slight variations in their thought process OR you only ever talk to the "sales lawyer" and not the person who will represent you. You find yourself buying books and reading a lot of information. At some point, you have to trust yourself, trust the universe, and just retain someone.

Now, here is a solid piece of advice I CAN give you. When you first start calling lawyers, especially for California, there is only a ten-day window to get in touch with the DMV after your arrest in order to hold off the suspension of your license and schedule a hearing. If you don't know that, you're screwed. If you do know that, you feel pressured to hire someone right away. Now, I made the mistake of hiring someone too quickly. They had the initial contact with the DMV, but then things changed, and the person I initially spoke to was not the one who was going to represent me. I was not feeling good about the relationship. I ended up having to release them of their representation and search for someone I felt comfortable talking to. That was tough, but at least the urgent matter of the DMV got taken care of. Making sure I made the right decision the second time around was super tough.

I went from making a rash decision to dragging out endless research. I'm sure there is a happy medium somewhere, but when your reputation, your new business, your nursing license, driving license, and criminal record are all on the line, it's not a decision to take lightly or just take the first person who calls you back. You need someone who knows the law and can hopefully make an impression with the spirit of the law versus the letter of the law. That is a term I learned long ago when I was married to the CHP officer. That terminology was also used by the first law office I hired and partially why I felt comfortable with them initially. However, the second lawyer I hired was not familiar with that terminology. That alone almost made me turn away. Again, I should have gone with my instinct.

The person who referred me to the second lawyer was terribly insulting to me when I asked him a general question after our initial consultation before I retained him. Sometimes it's good to talk to someone twice so you see their true colors. He was so nice the first time but turned from Dr. Jekyll into Mr. Hyde the second time we spoke. I could only sit on the phone, let him literally yell at me, and say, "Yes, sir…no, sir." As if you aren't in enough of a predicament already, with plenty of people insulting and yelling at you. Then you have to deal with someone who should be on your side doing the same thing. DON'T hire that person.

His referral, however, seemed quite different. I could tell he had strength in criminal law. As well, his openness to alternative possibilities was favorable. He seemed to be someone who was collaborative with others as needed as well as with you, the client. Those are very important qualities.

However, I still could not get over the fact that his referral treated me the way he did. I decided to leave that lawyer as well because I had a bad feeling about how differently he treated me from the consultation versus getting down to business. Your lawyer should be consistent. The first conversation should not be a sales pitch with subsequent communication being drastically different.

It really takes several contacts with someone before you can make the right decision. The second lawyer, who was referred by the person who yelled at me, was not giving me a good feeling once I paid the deposit. So, I continued to review lawyers and had yet more conversations. When you follow your intuition, you WILL find the right one.

Where does it end? Now that I have let the second lawyer go, he will not return the $2,000 I gave him and is completely ignoring me. It's like an unhealthy romantic relationship - You never know what that person is really like until you break up with them. I am not suggesting you hire people and then un-hire them to see what happens. What I am suggesting is that you really need to feel GREAT about who you are hiring. Do not pay or put down a full retainer until you have talked to enough lawyers and made several contacts with the list you have narrowed down.

Don't go with someone who is so egotistical that they yell at you if you ask them a strategy question.

Don't go with someone who is not willing to communicate with you directly, especially for the consultation. Don't go with someone if they do not know more than one strategy or are not open to various options of defense. Every situation is different. There is not a "one size fits all" way to handle these cases. Do your homework, know your defense options, and be sure that whoever you chose is willing to explore whatever option applies to your specific situation. The more lawyers you talk to, the more you will know what questions to ask and what to look for in a lawyer. My suggestion would be to have your initial conversation, then a few days later, call back with a general question. It's how they handle the second call that is the best gauge. Always make sure you have a direct conversation with the person who is actually representing you. I did converse with two agencies whose initial contact was NOT with my litigation lawyer. One firm never called back when I wanted to talk to the lawyer who was going to represent me. This whole process was trial and error. Learn from my errors. (Especially the one about never drinking and driving!)

I bring this up in the book because now, my life depends on this key decision. I can only hope this lawyer understands that if I cannot drive in California, I get this criminal charge on my record, and I am disciplined by the board, my life is over. Everyone deserves forgiveness and a close look at the uniqueness of the situation as well as the spirit of the law. Humans are subject to human error, and machines such as breathalyzers are subject as well to errors.

Once you think you have made the right decision, still leave some time (a day or so) to let it all sink in, then follow your intuition. Make a pros and cons list. This is NOT an easy decision. Your future and life depend on this decision.

Once you go through all this, you need to find a different lawyer who can handle the Board that you are licensed with. You do have to go through this whole process AGAIN in order to find that lawyer. Finding one is the same process as finding DUI defense. You have to talk to a lot of them and find one who fits what you believe, who will defend you in the same manner, and one with the same philosophy, same principles, and empathy of a nurse, but most of all, one that is very experienced. The more you speak with, the better discernment you will have. Here is what I know to date. The board is going to send you a letter that you have to respond to within fourteen days. If you don't respond or respond the way I did (which was talked about earlier in this book), they will send you a second letter saying you have to respond within five days of that second letter.

The truth is that the Nursing Board cannot do anything until you have gone through the legal system. These letters are scare tactics. (However, if you have a problem with alcohol or drugs, take advantage of what they are offering and go through their diversion program.) After you hire your criminal lawyer, take your time and find the right BRN lawyer. I called and spoke to six lawyers who were specific to BRN law. Don't speak to the ones who want to charge you full price for a consultation fee. There are plenty who will speak to you without charging. The lawyers who want to charge you know that you don't need them until after the court case is settled. That is why they won't give a free consultation; they want to get paid for a full hour of consultation now because they know you won't need them for at least a few more months. You don't need a lawyer until you have the court's final decision. Then your lawyer should contact the Board within thirty days.

Chapter 8

Misconceptions and Myths Versus Reality

There are many misconceptions about using alcohol and driving. Below are some common myths that HG.org Legal Resources has taken the time to debunk.[4]

Water or Coffee Diminishes the Effect of Alcohol

Some people drink to excess and think that if they simply splash water on their face or have a cup of coffee that they will not be impaired by alcohol. While these tactics may help a person stay awake and may help him or her avoid falling asleep at the

---

[4] *Hg.org*, www.hg.org/legal-articles/dispelling-misconceptions-about-dui-39878.

wheel, they will not influence the person's level of impairment. It takes time for the effects caused by drinking to wear off.

Breathalyzer Tests are Completely Accurate

Some people believe that breathalyzer tests are completely accurate and that there are no plausible reasons for a false reading. This may influence them to plead guilty because they believe they committed the crime. However, breathalyzer tests are fallible.

There are a number of factors that can affect the accuracy of a breathalyzer reading. The machine has to be periodically inspected and calibrated or the readings can be off. The test must be properly administered. Many times, the person operating the machine may have limited experience and may not properly administer the test. Environmental factors can impact the reading. Additionally, medical conditions or food intake can impact the results of a breathalyzer test.

Any Lawyer Can Handle a DUI Case

Avoid making this mistake. DUI cases involve specialized knowledge and a familiarity with the processes involved in investigating DUI suspects and in collecting test samples. A DUI lawyer knows what information to challenge. He or she cannot be substituted by a lawyer unfamiliar with this area of law.

Chapter 9

That's What's Left in your Bank Account When This is Over

I know I spoke about costs in the beginning; however, there are some additional details and points to be made on that front.

The Cost Comparison of Getting a DUI

Comparison of what "they" say the costs are vs. what the costs really are.

The following are costs as found on "How Much Does a DUI Really Cost? $10,000? 15,000?":[5]

---

[5] Torrance, and S.a. "How Much Does a DUI Really Cost? $10,000? $15,000?" *Los Angeles County DUI Lawyers Greg Hill & Associates*, www.greghillassociates.com/how-much-does-a-dui-really-cost-10-000-15-000.html.

Towing / Impound Fees for Vehicle	$500
Attorney fees	$3,000 (can range quite a bit)
DMV fees	$125 (license reissue fee)
Ignition Interlock Device (IID) fees	$300 (varies by device)
Booking fees	$330 (varies by city)
Court fines, penalties & assessments	$1,950 ($390 base fine)
Alcohol awareness classes	$650 (3, 6 or 9 month, varies)
Mothers Against Drunk Driving Class	$35
Hospital and Morgue (HAMM) Class	$120
Lost earnings due to classes, court	$1,500 (varies by person)
Added car insurance premiums over 3 years.	$4,500 (varies by insurer)
Total:	**$13,010**

Here is the reality of the situation from one incident of driving over 0.08%. These are actual numbers based on my situation.

Towing / Impound Fees for Vehicle	$600-$1000
Attorney fees if no trial	$3,000- $6500
Attorney Fees if there's a trial	$5000-$10,000 ***_additional_
(most cases don't go to trial; however, withall that is at stake for you as a professional, you may seriously want to consider this.)	
The Attorney you are going to need to defend your RN license	$5000-$10,000 *** _additional_
The BRN Diversion Program	$10,000-$50,000 ***_for "voluntary" participation_
DMV fees	$125 (license reissue fee)
Ignition Interlock Device (IID) fees	$300 (varies by device)
Booking fees	$330 (varies by city)
Court fines, penalties & assessments	$1,950 ($390 base fine)
Alcohol awareness classes	$650 (3, 6 or 9 month, varies)
Mothers Against Drunk Driving Class	$35
Hospital and Morgue (HAMM) Class	$120

Lost earnings due to classes, court	$1,500 (varies by person)
Added car insurance premiums over 3 years	$4,500 (varies by insurer)
Total:	**$28,110 - $92,010**

Those are some _SCARY_ numbers. Frightening numbers. In fact, as of writing this book, I am only at the attorney fee part of the equation. I don't know what I am in for with the rest of it. I'm terrified. I have no family, no husband, and no one to ask for money. I won't be able to work as a nurse, so what's left? I can sell my house and move into a rental to get the equity I need for the money. However, moving from a home where I pay $836 mortgage compared to $1400 rent seems like a punishment way above and beyond the punishment that fits the crime.

I was surprised to find numbers on the internet by law enforcement or lawyers themselves professing such low values. My numbers quickly added up to their overall number, even before any DMV or court hearing. Keep that in mind. Whatever you see on the internet - DOUBLE it!

Chapter 10

How to Avoid Getting a DUI/DWI

Don't drive, even if you have only had one drink.
It doesn't take much to go over the limit. I'm a little older and from the school of thought that having one drink an hour and pacing yourself will keep you within the limits of the law. Things are changing now. People are being educated that there are no hard and fast rules and the only way to avoid an incident is to simply NOT drive if you have a drink. Based on my experience, I would have to agree.

If you are only going to have ONE drink, you probably don't really need to have that drink. Wait until you get home. Ultimately, the cost of a cab, Uber, or any other arrangement is unequivocally the better option than facing any potential consequences of a police encounter.

Remember, that an encounter with police can occur even if there is no accident or you are not driving erratically. What if someone hits you? Even if that person is totally at fault and not drinking, if you have been drinking, you may be seen as responsible. The person with alcohol on their breath is NOT given the benefit of the doubt. Take all the money I spent on this DUI so far, and I would have cab fare for life. In fact, I could buy a car and hire a driver. You just saw the reality of the numbers in the previous chapter, so you do the math.

So, how does one avoid a DUI?

The best way to avoid getting a DUI is to leave your car at home. Then you have no temptation to drive home at all, and no one can ask you for a ride home.

The issue with where I live is that public transportation is not readily available. I cannot afford to live anywhere else. If I could call Uber or Lyft, you damn well know I would have. Whenever I am somewhere that these rides are available, I use it. There is no public transportation here. When I went to Ireland, I LOVED public transportation. It was lovely not to have to drive. You get into the bus or train and you get work done, no stress of driving; it's beautiful. In America, we all know that public transportation is very limited and it takes you from point A to point B. It doesn't take most people from their *specific* point A to their *specific* point B. It's a quandary.

Remember, you have other options. Share a cab or have a designated driver. I have been the designated driver many times, and I have arranged for cabs prior to going out or after driving one way to where I am going. I have left my car at friends' houses that had me spend the night. I have insisted many times on paying the rides to and from places, so we would not have to worry about driving at all. Those are my usual practices.

My big idea has always been to have a fun bar for the community with games and lounge areas with a decked out van all painted up with the bar logo and other fun pictures and actually give people rides to and from the establishment. I would have designated bus stops so that most anyone could easily walk to the bus stop and easily walk home afterward from the bus stop. I don't know why more places don't do that in towns in which there is only ONE taxi service with literally one car. So why did I not practice my ultra safe driving techniques this time? There were a few reasons *WHY* I did not do any of that:

1. I went out alone (you can do that here because everyone knows everyone and it's safe in that way).
2. I did not go out with the intention of over-indulging. I just wanted to SING! (NO, I don't need liquid courage for that)
3. I offered to give someone a ride home because the nurse in me is a nurturer, and I help people who need help.
4. I felt OK to drive after pacing myself and drinking a lot of water.

There are SO many alternate scenarios that *could* have happened and this all would have been avoided:

1. First, I should have listened to my intuition and stayed home. The best option so far.

2. I should have never offered to give that person a ride home. I would have left the karaoke restaurant and driven right home.

3. If I had taken that person home directly from the Elks Club instead of after the karaoke place, the tree would not yet have fallen and been across the road.

4. If the CHP had the road closed properly and did not appear as "proceed with caution" if there was not a car ahead of me that turned onto the road, if I had not assessed the situation to discover that the lane was open where I had to turn, I would have not gone down that street avoiding this situation altogether.

If… If…If….The "If's" go on and on.

If you are determined to drive your car, buy a breathalyzer and keep it in your glove box. If you are over the limit, go back into the place, wait, and drink water. When I was out a long while back, a friend had a breathalyzer in their glove box. He was kind enough to let us all blow into it. I was a bit over. He escorted us back into the bar to have a large glass of ice water and just wait about thirty minutes. Sure enough, I was below the limit when we left the second time. I was grateful for that. Which is why I now have a breath machine in my car glove box. Unfortunately, I put it in the glove box after I was arrested.

Here are some other tips found on the website for the Duke Law Group[6]:

- **Eat before you drink.** A lack of food in your system causes you to become drunk much faster and it's also very risky, as this approach can lead to poor concentration, nutritional deficits, impaired judgment, and long-term serious health effects and diseases.
- **Set a limit.** Use a BAC calculator to determine an approximate amount of

---

[6] "8 Tips to Help Avoid Drunk Driving." *Duke Law Group*, 10 Sept. 2016, mi-dui-attorney.com/avoid-drunk-driving/.

alcohol that you can safely drink while staying under the legal limit to drive. Stick to your limit.

- **Pace your drinks**. Never drink more than one alcoholic beverage in an hour and stop drinking at least one hour before you anticipate driving.

- **Drink a glass of water or non-alcoholic beverage between each alcoholic drink.**

- **Only bring cash and limit the amount.** Only bring enough cash into the bar to pay for the drinks that you have set your limit at. Leave credit cards and extra cash in your vehicle in case you need to pay for a taxi later.

- **Avoid drinking shots.** The average amount of alcohol in one shot of liquor is approximately the same as a 12 oz. beer.

- **Have a backup ride.** Be prepared by saving the phone number to a cab company or designated driver service in your phone. Save the number as "1 driver" so that it is easy to find in your contacts after you have been drinking.

A Faulty System

I know people who drink and drive all the time. Every day. They make sure they get home before dark. That's their system. There is also another person who outright does not own a car and has other friends who ARE over the limit drinkers drive him. He doesn't care about the friend driving as long as he's in the passenger seat. Somehow, it seems to work for them. However, my life would never come to that.

I didn't try to use some tricky system. I felt fine and knew my friend shouldn't drive. The absolute 100% truth is that not only was I keeping track of what I drank, I did feel OK, and I KNOW that those two glasses of wine I had at the karaoke restaurant were standard by-the-book pours. They do not give a drop over what they are supposed to.

Where I live, the bars are as expensive as Los Angeles. This is a small town that some celebrities have second getaway homes in. However, everything else is much less expensive, and that is why I live where I do. It's affordable to live, just not to go out. Why can't a night out on the town be affordable?

I guess it's just as well. I'm back to staying home again. Just me, my cat, my TV, and my books. I'm going to settle for the fact that at mid-life, I won't be able to get a job or drive. Moving out of the country may be my only option. If you think I'm kidding, I'm not. As of this moment, my court and DMV dates are set for May. I am going to have to prepare for the worst. That is how I am seeing the outcome at this point. How will I live if I can't get a job?

Chapter 11

The Endless Consequences

If this happened to me in order to convey the seriousness of being branded with the scarlet letter, because I am an action taker and chose to get this story out in order to help other people avoid any of this, I guess it will be worth it.

The consequences of a DUI are the same, if not worse, than other Class A misdemeanors. Class A misdemeanors include a wide range of crimes, including burglary, assault resulting in injury, harboring a runaway child, conspiracy, and DUI. Somehow, putting a DUI without any accidents or other violations in this category seems like a **very severe penalty**.

In some ways, the consequences of a DUI are even worse. Some misdemeanors are more easily dropped or reduced. LegalMatch shares information on this for burglary cases:

> ### Can I Get a Burglary Sentence Dropped or Reduced?
>
> In many cases the defendant and their lawyer can make a request to have the charges dropped or the sentence reduced to a less severe one. Sometimes the court will take into other facts into consideration, such as the defendant's intentions in committing the burglary, and witness testimony supporting the defendant's overall good character.[7]

Can this happen in a DUI? To my knowledge, it's not the norm.

The consequences of this misdemeanor are life-destroying. First, if ever asked on a job application or on my professional license renewal if I have ever

---

[7] LaMance, Ken. "Penalties and Sentencing for Burglary." *LegalMatch Law Library*, 26 Feb. 2018, www.legalmatch.com/law-library/article/penalties-and-sentencing-for-burglary.html.

been arrested, I have to say YES. I will always be someone who has been arrested, REGARDLESS of the outcome of this.

Secondly, with the professional license, there are only two options at this point. Go into the BRN's 3-5 year program of rehabilitation (which is "voluntary") OR have a permanent mark on my record visible to the public of disciplinary action against my license. How can they say the program is voluntary if the outcome of not doing something voluntary will ruin the integrity of your license? The 3-5 year program is 10K a year from what I understand.

I will not be able to drive in the state where I reside for a long time. Three years is the punishment where a very expensive SR-22 (proof of liability insurance to the DMV) is required, not to mention your regular insurance going up. License suspension of a year or severely restricted to only to and from work. Where I live on this mountain, without public transportation or readily available taxi services, coupled with the fact that EVERYTHING is down the hill fifteen miles or more each way, not having the ability to drive poses a huge dilemma. How can you live if you can't grocery shop, go to the doctor, bring your animals to the vet, see clients for your business, or go to work if you still have a job?

The scarlet letter on your driver's license will remain for ten years at least. I am not certain if the laws have changed to make that an indefinite mark. Your criminal record will be forever tainted.

There are some fluctuations and extenuating circumstances for both. A good lawyer will be able to answer those questions specific to your circumstance.

The outcome with the court system is having a misdemeanor on your record. You are now forever and always a criminal. You pay for a lawyer, fines, classes, and go to AA meetings. When all is said and done, getting through the criminal court is by far the easiest part of this whole thing, and look at how devastating it is.

The impact this has on your job, getting future jobs, your professional license, your inability to drive and your criminal record are just as bad as if you robbed a bank. Except, if I were a professional bank robber instead of a Registered Nurse, I would not have a professional license at stake. Criminals of that nature have work programs to integrate criminals back into society. I am a professional whose life as I know it now is over. Do I have to move to another state where I can drive? Since most states are reciprocal in their sharing of information, there will be consequences in the new state of licensure, so moving is not necessarily an option to solve the driving issues.

Seriously, is moving out of the country an option? If you do that, you cannot work in another country; you must prove self-sufficiency.

There are not many viable options here, as you can see. With all sincerity, if you get arrested for drinking and driving, your life is over. The way I see it is that each entity (the DMV, BRN, and the criminal justice system) think they are each the only one. They each see a need to punish to the fullest extent in order for you to "learn your lesson."

As a professional, you are punished by three

entities without consideration of circumstances the way other misdemeanors are. Those three entities are the organization that gave you driving privileges, the organization that gives you the scarlet letter of "criminal," AND the organization that issued your hard-earned professional license. I was going to get a second job to pay for all of these additional expenses including publishing this book. I don't think I will be able to get one. I was called as a candidate to fill a position. One that I didn't even apply for. They came directly to me. I didn't follow through when I saw they did a full background check. It would be far too embarrassing to get "caught" with a "dirty" background check than to not do it at all.

Somehow you HAVE to instill in your psyche the depth of the crime that drinking over the limit of 0.08% is. That it's A CRIME, not to be messed with. You wouldn't walk into a store or restaurant and steal a bottle of wine if you didn't have the money. Consequences for a DUI/DWI are the SAME, if not worse. I cannot stress enough that you cannot operate a car if you are going to imbibe.

Life as I know it has changed forever. Everything I have worked for can be gone in an instant. Nursing license - gone. Driving license - gone.

Criminal record forever stamped with the scarlet letters:

DUI / DWI

Appendix A

Consequence for a Pilot:

If you received a DUI with a blood alcohol content less than 0.15; *and* you never refused to submit to blood alcohol testing; *and* you report it to the FAA as required; *and* you have had no other arrest or conviction at any other time, your medical examiner has the authority to issue an aviation medical certificate without involving the FAA.[8]

---

[8] Houston, Sarina. "What Happens When a Pilot Gets a DUI." *The Balance Small Business*, www.thebalancesmb.com/aviation-medical-exams-can-you-fly-after-a-dui-282924.

Consequence for a Police Officer:

In most cases, police officers guilty of DUIs while off-duty will keep their jobs if it is a one-time occurrence and followed up with appropriate disciplinary and rehabilitative actions. For example, a Vermont police officer with 15 years experience kept his job after pleading guilty to a DUI in which the officer had passed out in his truck. Often the officer is temporarily placed on administrative leave as occurred in the case of a 24-year veteran of the Pennsylvania State Police officer (and the officer in charge of DUI checkpoints) who was found passed out after hitting a guardrail. Sometimes the administrative leave (or suspension) is indefinite, during which time the officer submits to rehab. On occasion, police officers who commit DUIs are not arrested, but simply cited and released, supposedly to avoid putting the officer in jail with other inmates, as was the case with a Sun Valley assistant police chief busted with a .17 BAC.

In summary, as a very general rule, an officer

involved in a DUI while off duty in which there is only property damage is likely to remain employed as a police officer following either disciplinary action and/or temporary suspension.[9]

Consequence for a Commercial Drivers License (CDL)

Aside from the lower threshold for BAC levels, CDL-holders charged with impaired driving while on the job are subject to the same criminal law procedures as non-commercial DUI defendants. In addition to the lowered blood alcohol limit, DUI in a commercial vehicle can result in longer license suspension than traditional DUI. This can mean a loss of livelihood for a commercial driver.

Additionally, CDL-holders convicted of any traffic violation aside from parking offenses must notify his or her employer within 30 days,

---

[9] Stim, Richard. "What Happens When a Police Officer Gets a DUI?" *Dui.drivinglaws.org*, Nolo, 31 July 2014, dui.drivinglaws.org/resources/what-happens-when-a-police-officer-gets-dui.htm.

regardless of which vehicle was driven at the time. For example, a truck driver convicted of a DUI in his personal car while off duty must notify his employer. If the DUI results in a suspended or revoked license, his employer is barred from employing him as a driver for the duration of the license restriction. Those wishing to continue as commercial drivers can find it extremely difficult to secure employment with a DUI on their record.[10]

---

[10] "Commercial DUI Regulations." *Findlaw*, dui.findlaw.com/dui-charges/commercial-dui-regulations.html.

References

Hg.org, www.hg.org/legal-articles/dispelling-misconceptions-about-dui-39878.

"8 Tips to Help Avoid Drunk Driving." *Duke Law Group*, 10 Sept. 2016, mi-dui-attorney.com/avoid-drunk-driving/.

Bjerke, Benjamin. "Cervical Stenosis with Myelopathy." *Spine*, www.spine-health.com/conditions/spinal-stenosis/cervical-stenosis-myelopathy.

"Commercial DUI Regulations." *Findlaw*, dui.findlaw.com/dui-charges/commercial-dui-regulations.html.

Emoto, Masaru. *The Hidden Messages in Water*. Atria Books, 2005.

Houston, Sarina. "What Happens When a Pilot Gets a DUI." *The Balance Small Business*, www.thebalancesmb.com/aviation-medical-exams-can-you-fly-after-a-dui-282924.

LaMance, Ken. "Penalties and Sentencing for Burglary." *LegalMatch Law Library*, 26 Feb. 2018, www.legalmatch.com/law-library/article/penalties-and-sentencing-for-burglary.html.

Stim, Richard. "What Happens When a Police Officer Gets a DUI?" *Dui.drivinglaws.org*, Nolo, 31 July 2014, dui.drivinglaws.org/resources/what-happens-when-a-police-officer-gets-dui.htm.

Torrance, and S.a. "How Much Does a DUI Really Cost? $10,000? $15,000?" *Los Angeles County DUI Lawyers Greg Hill & Associates*, www.greghillassociates.com/how-much-does-a-dui-really-cost-10-000-15-000.html.

"What You Should Know About the BRN
Diversion Program." *SEIU Nurse Alliance of
California,*
www.nurseallianceca.org/2015/02/02/what-you-
should-know-about-the-brn-diversion-program/.

Resources

<u>Websites:</u>

AA - http://aa-intergroup.org/directory.php

DUI Lawyers - https://www.hg.org/law-firms/usa-dui.html

BRN Lawyers - There is an organization called RN Guardian. I cannot recommend anyone, however, look up RN Guardian and decide for yourself. They are an organization that can help a variety of situations with the board. They will also talk to you even if you aren't a member. I joined after all the good information they provided for me for free. https://rnguardian.com/the-diversion-program-pros-and-cons/

<u>Books:</u>

Breaking the Habit of Being Yourself by Dr. Joe Dispenza

This book combines the fields of quantum physics, neuroscience, brain chemistry, biology, and genetics to show you what is truly possible in life. You can make measurable changes. Nothing about your life is set in stone. This book will give you a new perspective on life and help you through life-altering events.

Radical Self Forgiveness by Colin Tipping

I needed this book in order to give myself the tools to forgive myself. This book comes with a website and worksheets that you walk through in accordance with the exercises in the book. It's WORK, but it is worth it.

www.ingramcontent.com/pod-product-compliance
Lightning Source LLC
Chambersburg PA
CBHW030015190526
45157CB00016B/2819